CELEBRATING TEACHERS

A Book of Appreciation

EDITED BY

CAROL KELLY-GANGI

and JUDE PATTERSON

BARNES
&NOBLE
BOOKS
NEW YORK

Acknowledgments

The editors wish to thank Ann Kashickey, Rage Kindelsperger,
Stephen Lynn, Stuart Miller, Gil Sanchez, Donna Sepkowski,
Rose Stallmeyer, Mo Stewart, and Sui Mon Wu for their
support, suggestions, and expertise.

To Mom and Dad with love—for all your years of patient teaching.
C.K.G.

To Rose Weddell Scherck, who lit the torch of my lifelong love
of language.
J.P.

2001 Barnes & Noble Books

ISBN 0-7607-2367-2

Book design by Leah Lococo

Illustrations by Paul Hoffman

Printed and bound in the United States of America

01 02 03 04 05 MC 9 8 7 6 5 4 3 2

KP

Introduction

Before we even take our first breath, we've begun a process that will continue every day of our lives. Learning. What we learn in the course of a lifetime—from both schools of higher learning and the school of hard knocks—runs the gamut from essential to frivolous, practical to lofty, and everything in between.

Celebrating Teachers warmly acknowledges the women and men who have dedicated their lives to helping us learn. Speakers of all kinds—from writers and poets to historians and humorists—offer their insights into learning, education, knowledge, and experience. From ancient Greece to 21st-century America, the book contains a veritable cornucopia of contributors weighing in on this weighty subject. There are pithy statements and pearls of wisdom from the likes of Mark Twain and Bill Gates, Helen Keller and Fred Rogers, Judy Blume and Woody Allen, Dylan Thomas and Thomas Wolfe. What do they have in common? In the words of fellow contributor Gilbert Highet, "Wherever there are beginners and experts, old and young, there is some kind of learning going on, and some sort of teaching. We are all pupils and we are all teachers."

Another group of contributors includes teachers and students from across the country who graciously participated in our web site surveys and have given us the benefit of their personal insights into teaching and learning. Teachers speak about what drew them to the profession—often a dynamic teacher who inspired them as students—and what keeps them in it today, despite all odds. They recount tales of challenging pupils, lessons students have taught them, humorous moments, and their biggest rewards. Students, on the other hand, recall their most memorable teachers, those they didn't appreciate until much later in life, and what their best teachers did to make school come alive for them.

Like a running narrative, the selections follow one another naturally, a dialogue that crosses the boundaries of time and place. What we hope comes through again and again is the great impact teachers have on their students. Aside from parents, they are without a doubt the most influential people in our most formative years. That teachers seem to recognize this influence and relish the opportunity to make a difference in the lives of their students is a testament to their vocation to teach.

When students were asked what they would say to their favorite teachers if they could contact them today, they almost unanimously replied, "Thank You." We hope this book echoes that sentiment—in thanking teachers for graciously giving of their time, their talents, and themselves.

—CAROL KELLY-GANGI AND JUDE PATTERSON

New York, NY and Kingston, NY, 2001

What office is there which involves more responsibility, which requires more qualifications, and which ought, therefore, to be more honourable, than that of teaching?

HARRIET MARTINEAU, *British writer and social critic*

He that teaches us anything which we knew not before is undoubtedly to be reverenced as a master.

SAMUEL JOHNSON, *British lexicographer and writer*

We should honor our teachers more than our parents, because while our parents cause us to live, our teachers cause us to live well.

PHILOXENUS, *Greek poet*

One mother can achieve more than a hundred teachers.

Jewish proverb

After successfully raising our three wonderful kids, teaching is an extension of motherhood for me. It is comforting to know that my nest will never be empty.

BARBARA JAMES, *Pittsburgh, Pennsylvania*

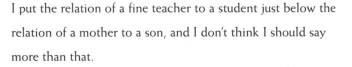

I put the relation of a fine teacher to a student just below the relation of a mother to a son, and I don't think I should say more than that.

THOMAS WOLFE, *American novelist*

I grew up living with my grandparents. Growing up without parents and always being the smallest and youngest kid in the class doesn't usually bode well for a student. But the teachers I had from grades one through twelve—and I still remember all of their names—made school a place where I could be at ease and where I was able to make many lifelong friends.

DENNIS CHICK, *Whitman, Massachusetts*

[Pupils] more willingly attend to one who gives directions than to one who finds faults.

QUINTILIAN, *Roman rhetorician*

Everywhere, we learn only from those whom we love.

JOHANN WOLFGANG VON GOETHE,

German poet and dramatist

A good teacher, like a good entertainer, first must hold his audience's attention. Then he can teach his lessons.

HENDRIK JOHN CLARKE, *American poet and editor*

Good teaching is one-fourth preparation and three-fourths theater.

GAIL GODWIN, *American writer*

What did your best teachers do to make a subject come alive for you?

Mr. Jones used to role-play some of the presidents. His portrayal of Andrew Jackson was particularly vivid and included chewing tobacco and a spitoon! I'll never forget his colorful description of President Jackson's inaugural party on the White House lawn.

Jolee Miles, Orlando, Florida

Mr. Green helped us love music in spite of ourselves. He taught the whole class to polka, without noting who was out of step, and he spent entire days teaching us Broadway musicals. He did not silence any of us, or stop us from dancing, so I smile remembering Carol Channing's "Hello, Dolly!" and sometimes I still sing "Oklahoma!" very loudly when I'm walking my dog.

Patricia Henking, Merrimack, New Hampshire

They didn't sit behind the desk—they moved around, flailed their arms, made faces, wrote on the board. I guess that's why I do those things when I teach. I tell my students— whatever it takes for you to learn. . . .

Debra Satchel, Thonotosassa, Florida

Monica Marcellus Winters taught English at my high school, and she was simply inspiring. We painted the walls of the classroom, had candlelit Dead Poets' Society meetings, and acted out the plays we were assigned to read—complete with costumes and props.

Kristina Aghassibake, College Station, Texas

When we studied the Civil War, we were divided into the North and the South. Every classroom had a masking tape Mason-Dixon line going down the middle of it. We had to sit on our respective sides with our army hats and patches everyday—we even assigned generals and sergeants. The entire wing of our school was completely engulfed in 1800s America. We learned a lot about ourselves that year.

Jennifer Benjamin, Cincinnati, Ohio

My Latin teacher, Michael Drialo, had an admirable balance of fun and seriousness in his classroom. Can you imagine making Latin FUN? He wasn't one to just go by the book—he related the subject in one way or another to our lives. We spent time learning why we studied Latin to begin with, its validity in the contemporary world, and how ancient history was applicable to the present day.

ShirleyAnn Tracy, Wells River, Vermont

Teachers provide a social and intellectual environment in which students can learn.

JAMES MACGREGOR BURNS, *American historian*

It is essential to enjoy the conditions of teaching, to feel at home in a room containing twenty or thirty healthy young people, and to make our enjoyment of this group-feeling give us energy for our teaching.

GILBERT HIGHET, *Scottish-born American classicist*

The truth is that I am enslaved . . . in one vast love affair with 70 children.

SYLVIA ASHTON-WARNER, *American teacher*

Housework is a breeze.
Cooking is a pleasant
diversion. Putting up a
retaining wall is a lark.
But teaching is like
climbing a mountain.

FAWN M. BRODIE, *American biographer*

I remember one time when I was having a very rough day. The kids weren't listening and didn't seem to be understanding anything. One girl came up to me and gave me a hug and said, "It'll be all right. We'll study really hard tonight and understand everything tomorrow."

JULIE FENNER, Pasadena, Texas

Teachers believe they have a gift for giving; it drives them with the same irrepressible drive that drives others to create a work of art or a market or a building.

A. BARTLETT GIAMATTI,
American educator and sports executive

I think, at a child's birth, if a mother could ask a fairy godmother to endow it with the most useful gift, that gift would be curiosity.

ELEANOR ROOSEVELT, American diplomat and writer

The whole art of teaching is only the art of awakening the natural curiosity of young minds for the purpose of satisfying it afterwards.

ANATOLE FRANCE, French writer

My fifth-grade teacher, Mrs. Hartung, took us into the
magical world of reading. We'd lay our heads down on our
desks, and she'd read to us about far away places. She gave us
hope that we could do anything, go anywhere, or be just
about anything our hearts desired.

NILA PUDWILL, *Bismarck, North Dakota*

No bubble is so iridescent or floats longer than that blown by
the successful teacher.

SIR WILLIAM OSLER, *Canadian physician*

Teaching is not a lost art, but the regard for it is a lost
tradition.

JACQUES BARZUN,

French-born American educator and historian

Teaching is an instinctual art, mindful of potential, craving of
realizations, a pausing, seamless process.

A. BARTLETT GIAMATTI,

American educator and sports executive

If you promise not to believe everything your child says happens at this school, I'll promise not to believe everything he says happens at home.

A British schoolmaster to his students' parents

Kids tell me about their parents' speeding tickets, messy houses, sisters' acne, and everything under the sun. But what touches me the most is when they tell me I'm their favorite teacher ever.

KELLY DEROSA, *Gilbert, Arizona*

The only reason I always try to meet and know the parents better is because it helps me to forgive their children.

LOUIS JOHANNOT, *Swiss headmaster*

Children have never been very good at listening to their elders, but they have never failed to imitate them.

JAMES BALDWIN, *American writer*

There must be such a thing as a child with average ability, but you can't find a parent who will admit that it is his child.

THOMAS BAILEY, *American educator*

The man who really knows can tell all that is transmissible in a very few words. The economic problem of the teacher (of violin or of language or of anything else) is how to string it out so as to be paid for more lessons.

EZRA POUND, *American poet*

One good teacher in a lifetime may sometimes change a delinquent into a solid citizen.

PHILIP WYLIE, *American writer*

When I see a child that everyone else has given up for lost succeed, my heart swells. I know that I am only a small part of the success but that is enough.

BONNIE HOSE, *Fairplay, Maryland*

Loving a child doesn't mean giving in to all his whims; to love him is to bring out the best in him, to teach him to love what is difficult.

NADIA BOULANGER, *French music teacher*

The best teacher I ever had was Mrs. Carol Downer. She made me realize that I wasn't going to be able to glide through life on my own terms—that eventually I was going to have to look at the big picture, not just through the tunnel vision of a teenager. She quite plainly told me to grow up, which is exactly what I needed to hear!

REBECCA GUIMONT, *Manchester, New Hampshire*

You have a wonderful child. Then, when he's 13, gremlins carry him away and leave in his place a stranger who gives you not a moment's peace. . . . You have to hang in there, because two or three years later, the gremlins will return your child, and he will be wonderful again.

JILL EIKENBERRY, *American actress*

In the first place God made idiots. This was for practice. Then He made School Boards.

MARK TWAIN, *American writer and humorist*

[T]he bearded bloke stepped to the footlights and started making a speech. From the fact that he spoke as if he had a hot potato in his mouth without getting a raspberry from the lads in the ringside seats, I deduced that he must be the headmaster.

P. G. WODEHOUSE, *English-born American writer*

It is easier for a tutor to command than to teach.

JOHN LOCKE, *British philosopher*

I maintain, in truth,

That with a smile we should instruct our youth,

Be very gentle when we have to blame,

And not put them in fear of virtue's name.

MOLIÈRE, *French dramatist*

If there is anything that we wish to change in the child, we should first examine it and see whether it is not something that could better be changed in ourselves.

CARL JUNG, *Swiss psychiatrist*

I came out of college so oriented on putting out great plays that I was very strict in my auditions. One year a freshman came to audition who I did not cast because he didn't fit my director's vision. He never came again. I saw him one day as a senior and asked him why he had never auditioned again. He very simply said, "You taught me I wasn't good enough." I was as hurt as he must have been. I never again blatantly turned away students; I always found a place for everyone who came.

LAURA LAMM, *Fayetteville, North Carolina*

I had learned to respect the intelligence, integrity, creativity and capacity for deep thought and hard work latent somewhere in every child; they had learned that I differed from them only in years and experience, and that as I, an ordinary human being, loved and respected them, I expected payment in kind.

SYBIL MARSHALL, *British teacher*

I have one rule—attention. They give me theirs and I give them mine.

SISTER EVANGELIST, R.S.M., *American teacher*

To know how to suggest is the great art of teaching. To attain it we must be able to guess what will interest; we must learn to read the childish soul as we might a piece of music. Then, by simply changing the key, we keep up the attraction and vary the song.

HENRI-FRÉDÉRIC AMIEL, *Swiss poet and philosopher*

Nobody can be taught faster than he can learn. . . . Every man that has ever undertaken to instruct others can tell what slow advances he has been able to make, and how much patience it requires to recall vagrant inattention, to stimulate sluggish indifference, and to rectify absurd misapprehension.

SAMUEL JOHNSON, *British lexicographer and writer*

Education is the ability to listen to almost anything without losing your temper or your self-confidence.

ROBERT FROST, *American poet and teacher*

I was not far into my first year teaching third graders. It was Christmastime so I decided to read *How the Grinch Stole Christmas* to the class. I was mentally patting myself on the back for doing such a great job when one student raised his hand. My bubble was deflated when he said, "It was better on TV." To this day, I try to stay humble because I know if I'm not, there will be a student to show me the truth!

JULEE JONES, *Antigo, Wisconsin*

The teacher should never lose his temper in the presence of the class. If a man, he may take refuge in profane soliloquies; if a woman, she may follow the example of one sweet-faced and apparently tranquil girl—go out in the yard and gnaw a post.

WILLIAM LYON PHELPS, *American educator*

The first idea that the child must acquire, in order to be actively disciplined, is that of the difference between *good* and *evil*; and the task of the educator lies in seeing that the child does not confound *good* with *immobility*, and *evil* with *activity*.

MARIA MONTESSORI, *Italian educator*

Iron rusts from disuse; stagnant water loses its purity and in cold weather becomes frozen; even so does inaction sap the vigour of the mind.

LEONARDO DA VINCI, *Italian artist and inventor*

Play is often talked about as if it were a relief from serious learning. But for children play is serious learning. Play is really the work of childhood.

FRED ROGERS, *American children's TV host*

My inspiration to teach grew from my own elementary days. We lived about seven miles from town and had no one near for playmates, so my sister and I acted out our school day each evening. My dad bought us a real blackboard, built us a chalk tray, and we were in business. I think, as I look back, I had no choice but to become a teacher.

BONNIE HOSE, *Fairplay, Maryland*

It is paradoxical that many educators and parents still differentiate between a time for learning and a time for play without seeing the vital connection between them.

LEO BUSCAGLIA, *American writer*

You must train the children to their studies in a playful manner, and without any air of constraint, with the further object of discerning more readily the natural bent of their respective characters.

PLATO, *Greek philosopher*

I see the mind of the 5-year-old as a volcano with two vents: destructiveness and creativeness.

SYLVIA ASHTON-WARNER, *American teacher*

It is the supreme art of
the teacher to awaken
joy in creative expression
and knowledge.

ALBERT EINSTEIN, *German-born American physicist*

In truth man is made rather to eat ices than to pore over old texts.

ANATOLE FRANCE, *French writer*

A child must feel the flush of victory and the heart-sinking of disappointment before he takes with a will to the tasks distasteful to him and resolves to dance his way through a dull routine of textbooks.

HELEN KELLER, *American writer and lecturer*

Knowledge can be communicated, but not wisdom.

HERMANN HESSE, *German-born Swiss novelist and poet*

The decent docent doesn't doze;
He teaches standing on his toes.
His student dassn't doze and does,
And that's what teaching is and was.

DAVID MCCORD,
American poet and Harvard fund-raiser

I think sleeping was my problem in school. If school had started at 4:00 in the afternoon, I'd be a college graduate today.

GEORGE FOREMAN, *American professional boxer*

I was allowed to ring the bell for five minutes until everyone was in assembly. It was the beginning of power.

JEFFREY ARCHER, *British politician and novelist*

From the first day in school until the day I graduated, everyone gave me one hundred plus in art. Well, where do you go in life? You go to the place where you got one hundred plus.

LOUISE NEVELSON, *Russian-born American sculptor*

My education was the liberty I had to read indiscriminately and all the time, with my eyes hanging out.

DYLAN THOMAS, *Welsh poet*

I owe everything to a system that made me learn by heart till I wept. As a result I have thousands of lines of poetry by heart. I owe everything to this.

GEORGE STEINER, *French-born American critic and novelist*

Sister Agnes Joseph, my fifth-grade teacher, taught me how to write. Now, whenever I spot a mistake in spelling or grammar, it seems as if the mistake pops up and slaps me. I can't overlook it due to the training that I received from her.

PAM JAVADI, *North Arlington, New Jersey*

One attraction of Latin is that you can immerse yourself in the poems of Horace and Catullus without fretting over how to say, "Have a nice day."

PETER BRODIE, *American teacher*

Every man with a bellyful of the classics is an enemy to the human race.

HENRY MILLER, *American novelist*

Study history, study history. In history lies all the secrets of statecraft.

WINSTON CHURCHILL, *British statesman*

The very concept of history implies the scholar and the reader. Without a generation of civilized people to study history, to preserve its records, to absorb its lessons and relate them to its own problems, history, too, would lose its meaning.

GEORGE F. KENNAN, *American educator*

When we . . . learn that this country and the western world have no monopoly of goodness and truth or of skills and scholarship, we begin to appreciate the ingredients that are indispensable to making a better world. In a life of learning that is, perhaps, the greatest lesson of all.

JOHN HOPE FRANKLIN, *American historian*

Human history becomes more and more a race between education and catastrophe.

H. G. WELLS, *British writer and political philosopher*

Stand firm in your refusal to remain conscious during algebra. In real life, I assure you, there is no such thing as algebra.

FRAN LEBOWITZ, *American journalist*

It is hard to convince a high school student that he will encounter a lot of problems more difficult than those of algebra and geometry.

EDGAR WATSON HOWE, *American editor and writer*

My favorite teacher was my sixth-grade teacher, Mrs. Carol Hone. She taught me that not all teachers are there to teach you just what's in the books, but also about life.

LAURA LINK, *Celina, Ohio*

In my early life, and probably even today, it is not sufficiently understood that a child's education should include at least a rudimentary grasp of religion, sex, and money. Without a basic knowledge of these three primary facts in a normal human being's life—subjects which stir the emotions, create events and opportunities, and if they do not wholly decide must greatly influence an individual's personality—no human being's education can have a safe foundation.

PHYLLIS BOTTOME, *British writer*

I've studied now Philosophy

And Jurisprudence, Medicine—

And even, alas! Theology—

From end to end with labor keen;

And here, poor fool! with all my lore

I stand, no wiser than before.

JOHANN WOLFGANG VON GOETHE,

German poet and dramatist

"I couldn't afford to learn [washing]," said the Mock Turtle
with a sigh. "I only took the regular course. . . . Reeling and
Writhing, of course, . . . and then the different branches of
Arithmetic—Ambition, Distraction, Uglification, and
Derision."

LEWIS CARROLL, *British writer and mathematician*

It is no matter what you teach them first, any more than what leg you shall put into your breeches first.

SAMUEL JOHNSON, *British lexicographer and writer*

Technology is just a tool. In terms of getting the kids working together and motivating them, the teacher is the most important.

BILL GATES, *American entrepreneur*

More important than the curriculum is the question of the methods of teaching and the spirit in which the teaching is given.

BERTRAND RUSSELL, *British philosopher and social critic*

Teachers, what has teaching taught you?

I've learned that teaching children to think and wonder is more important than learning a list of facts.

Nancy Garrelts, Duluth, Georgia

I think I expect more from my students than I used to. I've learned that the more you expect, and require, the more they give you. If they know you care enough to demand a lot from them, then they are more apt to do their best.

Valerie Stanley, Knoxville, Tennessee

When I began teaching, I was going to change the world or at least try to make it better. Some days it is enough just to get through. But then there are days that will remain forever golden in my memory. The day that my deaf student finally got an A on his spelling test; the day that my antisocial girl offered a pencil to her classmate. Times like this are proof that I'm not going to change the world one iota—my students are. That is a most humbling thought!

Bonnie Hose, Fairplay, Maryland

There *is* only one curriculum, no matter what the method of education: what is basic and universal in human experience and practice, the underlying structure of culture.

PAUL GOODMAN, *American literary critic*

All experience is an arch, to build upon.

HENRY BROOKS ADAMS, *American historian*

My bedroom was a chemistry laboratory. I would do experiments. Many a time the experiments would catch fire and I'd throw them out of the window. My mother would say, "Why are these curtains burning?" As soon as I got to university, I went from being a slug, not even a chrysalis, into a butterfly because I got to do what I wanted to do.

V. CRAIG JORDAN, *American cancer research scientist*

A guidance counselor who has made a fetish of security, or who has unwittingly surrendered his thinking to economic determinism, may steer a youth away from his dream of becoming a poet, an artist, a musician or any other of thousands of things, because it offers no security, it does not pay well, there are no vacancies, it has no "future."

HENRY M. WRISTON, *American educator*

We shall never learn to feel and respect our real calling and destiny, unless we have taught ourselves to consider every thing as moonshine, compared with the education of the heart.

SIR WALTER SCOTT, *Scottish poet and novelist*

Study, learn, but guard the original naïveté. It has to be within you, as desire for drink is within the drunkard or love is within the lover.

HENRI MATISSE, *French artist*

Every child is an artist. The problem is how to remain an artist once he grows up.

PABLO PICASSO, *Spanish artist*

Something awful happens to a person who grows up as a creative kid and suddenly finds no creative outlet as an adult.

JUDY BLUME, *American writer*

Education in our times must try to find whatever there is in students that might yearn for completion, and to reconstruct the learning that would enable them autonomously to seek that completion.

ALLAN BLOOM, *American educator and writer*

My mother always said that you should try everything at least once. She was very big on exposure and broadening our horizons. She said, "If I give them enough things to become interested in, first of all, it will keep them out of trouble, but also they will be better equipped to decide what they want to do when they get older."

RENEE ROBINSON, *American athlete and dancer*

The important thing is not so much that every child should be taught, as that every child should be given the wish to learn.

SIR JOHN LUBBOCK, *British financier and naturalist*

Thank you to Bob Adams, sophomore English teacher at Columbus High School, 1987, for teaching me to question, reason, wonder, explore, think outside of the box, and to never stop learning.

CINDY HEDGECOCK, *Denver, Colorado*

[It was] an initiation into the love of learning, of learning how to learn, that was revealed to me by my BLS [Boston Latin School] masters as a matter of interdisciplinary cognition—that is, learning to know something by its relation to something else.

LEONARD BERNSTEIN, *American composer and conductor*

If you are truly serious abut preparing your child for the future, don't teach him to subtract—teach him to deduct.

FRAN LEBOWITZ, *American journalist*

Without education, you are not going anywhere in this world.

MALCOLM X, *American political activist*

College is a refuge from hasty judgment.

ROBERT FROST, *American poet and teacher*

At college age, you can tell who is best at taking tests and going to school, but you can't tell who the best people are. That worries the hell out of me.

BARNABY C. KEENEY, *American educator*

The world's great men have not commonly been great scholars, nor its great scholars great men.

OLIVER WENDELL HOLMES SR.,
American physician and writer

Integrity without knowledge is weak and useless, and knowledge without integrity is dangerous and dreadful.

SAMUEL JOHNSON, *British lexicographer and writer*

The function of the university is not simply to teach bread-winning, or to furnish teachers for the public schools or to be a centre of polite society; it is, above all, to be the organ of that fine adjustment between real life and the growing knowledge of life, an adjustment which forms the secret of civilization.

W. E. B. DU BOIS, *American civil rights leader*

The importance of these [college] years for an American cannot be overestimated. They are civilization's only chance to get to him.

ALLAN BLOOM, *American educator and writer*

I was a modest, good-humoured boy. It is Oxford that has made me insufferable.

MAX BEERBOHM, *British caricaturist and writer*

If we have to have an exam at 11, let us make it one for humour, sincerity, imagination, character—and where is the examiner who could test such qualities.

A. S. NEILL, *Scottish-born British educator*

Examinations are formidable even to the best prepared, for the greatest fool may ask more than the wisest man can answer.

C. C. COLTON, *British writer and clergyman*

I was thrown out of N.Y.U. my freshman year . . . for cheating on my metaphysics final. You know, I looked within the soul of the boy sitting next to me.

WOODY ALLEN, *American filmmaker*

Do not on any account attempt to write on both sides of the paper at once.

W. C. SELLAR AND R. J. YEATMAN, *British writers*

The average Ph.D. thesis is nothing but a transference of bones from one graveyard to another.

JAMES FRANK DOBIE, *American historian*

The first duty of a university is to teach wisdom, not a trade; character, not technicalities. We want a lot of engineers in the modern world, but we don't want a world of engineers.

WINSTON CHURCHILL, *British statesman*

One by one the solid scholars

Get the degrees, the jobs, the dollars.

W. D. SNODGRASS, *American poet*

Term, holidays, term, holidays, till we leave school, and then work, work, work till we die.

C. S. LEWIS, *British writer*

I find the three major administrative problems on a campus are sex for the students, athletics for the alumni, and parking for the faculty.

CLARK KERR, *American educational reformer*

I read Shakespeare and the Bible and I can shoot dice. That's what I call a liberal education.

TALLULAH BANKHEAD, *American actress*

I was brought up to believe that the only thing worth doing was to add to the sum of accurate information in the world.

MARGARET MEAD, *American anthropologist*

To be possessed of a vigorous mind is not enough; the prime requisite is rightly to apply it.

RENÉ DESCARTES, *French mathematician and philosopher*

Four years was enough of Harvard. I still had a lot to learn but had been given the liberating notion that now I could teach myself.

JOHN UPDIKE, *American novelist*

The aim of the college, for the individual student, is to eliminate the need in his life for the college; the task is to help him become a self-educating man.

C. WRIGHT MILLS, *American sociologist*

A man must always study, but he must not always go to school: what a contemptible thing is an old abecedarian!

MONTAIGNE, *French essayist*

No one can "get" an education, for of necessity education is a continuing process.

LOUIS L'AMOUR, *American novelist*

Any place that anyone can learn something useful from someone with experience is an educational institution.

AL CAPP, *American cartoonist*

And let a scholar all Earth's volumes carry,
He will be but a walking dictionary.

GEORGE CHAPMAN, *British translator of classic literature*

As the biggest library if it is in disorder is not as useful as a small but well-arranged one, so you may accumulate a vast amount of knowledge but it will be of far less value to you than a much smaller amount if you have not thought it over for yourself.

ARTHUR SCHOPENHAUER, *German philosopher*

Depend upon it there comes a time when for every addition of knowledge you forget something that you knew before. It is of the highest importance, therefore, not to have useless facts elbowing out the useful ones.

SIR ARTHUR CONAN DOYLE, *British writer*

The most useful piece of learning for the uses of life is to unlearn what is untrue.

ANTISTHENES, *Greek philosopher*

Education consists mainly in what we have unlearned.

MARK TWAIN, *American writer and humorist*

It is only when we forget all our learning that we begin to know.

HENRY DAVID THOREAU, *American writer and naturalist*

Education is what survives when what has been learnt has been forgotten.

B. F. SKINNER, *American psychologist*

The first rule of intelligent tinkering is to save all the parts.

PAUL RALPH EHRLICH, *American biologist*

Most of the most important experiences that truly educate cannot be arranged ahead of time with any precision.

HAROLD TAYLOR, *American educator*

The best-educated human being is the one who understands most about the life in which he is placed.

HELEN KELLER, *American writer and lecturer*

To the best of my knowledge there has been no child in space. I would like to learn about being weightless, and I'd like to get away from my mother's cooking.

JONATHAN ADASHEK,

age 12, in a letter to President Ronald Reagan

I cannot join the space program and restart my life as an astronaut, but this opportunity to connect my abilities as an educator with my interests in history and space is a unique opportunity to fulfill my early fantasies.

CHRISTA MCAULIFFE, *American teacher*

I'm never going to be a movie star. But then, in all probability, Liz Taylor is never going to teach first and second grade.

MARY J. WILSON, *American teacher*

I'd never try to learn from someone I didn't envy at least a little. If I never envied, I'd never learn.

BETSY COHEN, *American therapist*

Everyone should learn to do one thing supremely well because he likes it, and one thing supremely well because he detests it.

B. W. M. YOUNG, *British headmaster*

How could youths better learn to live than by at once trying the experiment of living?

HENRY DAVID THOREAU, *American writer and naturalist*

Do you know the difference between education and experience? Education is what you get when you read the fine print. Experience is what you get when you don't.

PETE SEEGER, *American folk singer*

The person who has had a bull by the tail once has learned 60 or 70 times as much as a person who hasn't.

MARK TWAIN, *American writer and humorist*

We cannot learn without pain.

ARISTOTLE, *Greek philosopher*

For a man to attain to an eminent degree in learning costs him time, watching, hunger, nakedness, dizziness in the head, weakness in the stomach, and other inconveniences.

MIGUEL DE CERVANTES, *Spanish writer*

This life's hard, but it's harder if you're stupid.

GEORGE V. HIGGINS, *American novelist*

If you think education is expensive, try ignorance.

DEREK BOK, *American educator (attributed)*

Experience keeps a dear school, but fools will learn in no other.

BENJAMIN FRANKLIN, *American philosopher and diplomat*

There are some people that if they don't know, you can't tell 'em.

LOUIS ARMSTRONG, *American jazz musician*

For every person who wants to teach there are approximately thirty who don't want to learn—much.

W. C. SELLAR AND R. J. YEATMAN, *British writers*

Who was a teacher that you didn't appreciate until much later in life?

My typing teacher. I sure didn't appreciate her at the time, but I have used what she taught me all of my life. Thanks Mabel.
Jim Sumner, Derby, Kansas

For me, it would be Mrs. Cyr from high school. She taught history, and I was no history fan. I passed the class on sheer grace, but now I wish that I'd paid more attention and knew more about our country's history, not only for my sake, but for my children's as well.
Melinda Kiper, Tallahassee, Florida

My chorus teacher, Mr. Ray. He quietly and gently made us appreciate music as a whole, and taught us that we don't have to love every type of music but that we should respect the differences of each—which is a lesson that can be carried over into ALL aspects of life!
Rebecca Guimont, Manchester, New Hampshire

Mrs. Hall, my art teacher. At the time, I didn't think art mattered. She used to say that we come in all kinds to weave the fabric of the world. Now I get it.

Connie Rogerson, Springdale, Washington

I didn't appreciate my fifth-grade teacher. She was strict and demanded more than what was required. Instead of the usual 20-word spelling test, she would give 50- and even 100-word tests. I was a poor speller, but when Ms. Goodine got through with me, I was able to hold my own. Thanks, Ms. Goodine. Life and time have justifed your methods.

Jake Nixon, New York, New York

A teacher that I didn't appreciate until much later in life would be Mrs. Grega. I never thought she was a very good teacher until a while ago, when I realized if it hadn't been for her I would never have learned how to draw heads.

Kaitlin Patterson, age 14, Kingston, New York

The great difficulty in education is to get experience out of ideas.

GEORGE SANTAYANA, *Spanish-born American philosopher*

Training is everything. The peach was once a bitter almond; cauliflower is nothing but cabbage with a college education.

MARK TWAIN, *American writer and humorist*

The roots of education are bitter, but the fruit is sweet.

ARISTOTLE, *Greek philosopher*

Folks don't like to have somebody around knowin' more than they do. It aggravates 'em. You're not gonna change any of them by talkin' right, they've got to want to learn themselves, and when they don't want to learn there's nothing you can do but keep your mouth shut or talk their language.

HARPER LEE, *American writer*

I do not open up the truth to one who is not eager to get knowledge. . . . When I have presented one corner of a subject to anyone, and he cannot from it learn the other three, I do not repeat my lesson.

CONFUCIUS, *Chinese philosopher*

Teachers open the door, but you must enter by yourself.

Chinese proverb

When I find the road narrow, and can see no other way of teaching a well established truth except by pleasing one intelligent man and displeasing ten thousand fools—I prefer to address myself to the man.

MAIMONIDES, *Spanish-born rabbi*

The Master said, Yu, shall I teach you what knowledge is? When you know a thing, to recognize that you know it, and when you do not know a thing, to recognize that you do not know it. That is knowledge.

CONFUCIUS, *Chinese philosopher*

Knowledge is the recognition of something absent; it is a
salutation, not an embrace.

GEORGE SANTAYANA, *Spanish-born American philosopher*

I am sufficiently proud of my knowing something to be
modest about my not knowing everything.

VLADIMIR NABOKOV, *Russian-born American novelist*

If most of us are ashamed of shabby clothes and shoddy
furniture, let us be more ashamed of shabby ideas and shoddy
philosophies.

ALBERT EINSTEIN, *German-born American physicist*

There are no dangerous thoughts; thinking itself is dangerous.

HANNAH ARENDT, *German-born American political scientist*

To be able to be caught up into the world of thought—that is educated.

EDITH HAMILTON, *German-born American classicist*

In the realm of ideas it is better to let the mind sally forth, even if some precious preconceptions suffer a mauling.

ROBERT F. GOHEEN, *American educator*

Every act of conscious learning requires the willingness to suffer an injury to one's self-esteem. That is why young children, before they are aware of their own self-importance, learn so easily; and why older persons, especially if vain or important, cannot learn at all.

THOMAS SZASZ, *Hungarian-born American psychiatrist*

A child of five would understand this. Send someone to fetch a child of five.

GROUCHO MARX, *American actor and comedian*

Teachers, what keeps teaching worthwhile for you?

There's nothing like the look that a child gets when understanding really hits them. It's like watching a sunrise up close.

Sheldon Jonas, Bensonhurst, New York

The kids, without a doubt. I have taught seventh grade for fifteen years. When some would groan about thirteen year olds, I smile. They are unpredictable, enjoyable, sociable, and most of the time a joy to teach and to know.

Lynne Gibson, Elkins Park, Pennsylvania

Having a student from years' past hail me in a store with a hug and a "remember me?" Wow, in some small way I have touched that child. Now, THAT'S immortality!

Bonnie Hose, Fairplay, Maryland

Watching kids accomplish goals they never dreamed possible.

Daniel Slowik, Sunrise, Florida

There is nothing more satisfying than a child experiencing that "Aha" moment. "I get it now!" they exclaim with a great big grin, and you know you've been part of the process.
Norma Horan, Hilliard, Ohio

The twenty smiling faces that come into my room every morning and the sad faces that don't want to leave at the end of the year!
Jennifer Francone, Visalia, California

All that I learn from my students—about life, literature, and learning. They bring me experiences, laughter, insight, and observations. The students complement the learning I have already acquired, and keep my days rich and curious.
Dawna Buchanan, Warrensburg, Missouri

For my forty-year teaching career, I always loved the wit and the spirit of children.
Joyce Mills, Becklet, West Virginia

My kids. I touch the future through my students.
Amy Bonilla, Glendale, Arizona

Knowledge—like the sky—is never private property. No teacher has a right to withhold it from anyone who asks for it. Teaching is the art of sharing.

ABRAHAM JOSHUA HESCHEL,
Polish-born American theologian

To know is nothing at all; to imagine is everything.

ANATOLE FRANCE, *French writer*

Knowledge is a polite word for dead but not buried
imagination.

E. E. CUMMINGS, *American poet*

Imagination is more important than knowledge. Knowledge is
limited. Imagination encircles the world.

ALBERT EINSTEIN, *German-born American physicist*

He who has imagination without learning has wings and
no feet.

JOSEPH JOUBERT, *French ethicist and essayist*

He who wishes to teach us a truth should not tell it to us, but simply suggest it with a brief gesture, a gesture which starts an ideal trajectory in the air along which we glide until we find ourselves at the feet of the new truth.

JOSÉ ORTEGA Y GASSET, *Spanish essayist and philosopher*

For rigorous teachers seized my youth,
And purged its faith, and trimmed its fire,
Showed me the high, white star of Truth,
There bade me gaze, and there aspire.

MATTHEW ARNOLD, *British poet and critic*

Knowledge is fostered by curiosity; wisdom is fostered by awe.

ABRAHAM JOSHUA HESCHEL,
Polish-born American theologian

Much learning does not teach understanding.

HERACLITUS, *Greek philosopher*

If a scholar have not faith (in his principles), how shall he take a firm hold of things?

MENCIUS, *Chinese Confucian philosopher*

It is better to have wisdom without learning than learning without wisdom.

C. C. COLTON, *British writer and clergyman*

Knowledge, if it does not determine action, is dead to us.

PLOTINUS, *Roman philosopher*

Our treasure lies in the beehive of our knowledge. We are perpetually on the way thither, being by nature winged insects and honey gatherers of the mind.

FRIEDRICH WILHELM NIETZSCHE,
German philosopher and poet

Books are the bees which carry the quickening pollen from one to another mind.

JAMES RUSSELL LOWELL, *American poet and editor*

What literature can and should do is change the people who teach the people who don't read the books.

A. S. BYATT, *British novelist*

If you cannot read all your books, at any rate handle them, and, as it were, fondle them. Let them fall open where they will. . . . Make a voyage of discovery, taking soundings of uncharted seas.

WINSTON CHURCHILL, *British statesman*

We shouldn't teach great books; we should teach a love of reading.

B. F. SKINNER, *American psychologist*

If we succeed in giving the love of learning, the learning itself is sure to follow.

SIR JOHN LUBBOCK, *British financier and naturalist*

The teacher who is attempting to teach without inspiring the pupil with a desire to learn is hammering on cold iron.

HORACE MANN, *American educator*

My favorite teacher was my fifth-grade teacher, Mrs. Ellenberger. She taught us with such kindness in a very strict Catholic school. She was very petite and had a slight physical handicap, but nothing could prevent the light and enthusiasm that she exuded. This enthusiasm was contagious, and it only made us want to learn more. She did not have to ask for respect from her students—it was given freely.

DONNA LISJACK, *Hampton, Virginia*

My European history teacher during my senior year of high school was exuberant and passionate about social change and feminism. She encouraged my free thinking, intellectual exploration, and risk-taking—and taught me that these things would ultimately matter much more than "fitting in" in high school.

JESSYE COHEN, *Richmond, Virginia*

Education is not
the filling of a pail,
but the lighting
of a fire.

WILLIAM BUTLER YEATS, *Irish poet*

We teach people how to remember, we never teach them how to grow.

OSCAR WILDE, *Irish-born British writer and wit*

We're drowning in information and starving for knowledge.

RUTHERFORD D. ROGERS, *American librarian*

Truth is the most valuable thing we have. Let us economize it.

MARK TWAIN, *American writer and humorist*

A teacher who can arouse a feeling for one single good action, for one single good poem, accomplishes more than he who fills our memory with rows and rows of natural objects, classified with name and form.

JOHANN WOLFGANG VON GOETHE,

German poet and dramatist

My favorite teacher was Mrs. Jones, a black woman in suburban New York. She taught us many things beyond the curriculum. Most of us were white kids living in suburbia. She opened our eyes to prejudice and injustice and inspired a passion for justice in many of us.

LYNNE GIBSON, *Elkins Park, Pennsylvania*

There can be no knowledge without emotion. We may be aware of a truth, yet until we have felt its force, it is not ours. To the cognition of the brain must be added the experience of the soul.

ARNOLD BENNETT, *British novelist*

Human beings are full of emotion, and the teacher who knows how to use it will have dedicated learners. It means sending dominant signals instead of submissive ones with your eyes, body and voice.

LEON LESSINGER, *American educator*

What a teacher doesn't say . . . is a telling part of what a
student hears.

MAURICE NATANSON, *American educator*

The mediocre teacher tells. The good teacher explains. The
superior teacher demonstrates. The great teacher inspires.

WILLIAM ARTHUR WARD, *British novelist*

I feel as though teaching is ten percent inspiration and ninety
percent divine call. Without that, the patience, perseverance,
and energy that teaching requires of you would disappear with
the shadow of the coming school year in August.

SUSAN SOARES, *Bristol, Rhode Island*

No man can reveal to you aught but that which already lies
half asleep in the dawning of your knowledge.

KAHLIL GIBRAN, *Lebanese-born American poet*

Language is a living, kicking, growing, flitting, evolving reality, and the teacher should spontaneously reflect its vibrant and protean qualities.

JOHN A. RASSIAS, *American educator*

Children have a natural talent for writing poetry and anyone who teaches them should know that. Teaching really is not the right word for what takes place: it is more like permitting the children to discover something they already have.

KENNETH KOCH, *American poet and teacher*

The best teacher I ever had was Ms. Angermeier. She taught me to love literature and language—her way of reciting poems was soul-touching. She taught me to respect and enjoy the beauty and meaning of words.

OSCAR SARAVIA, *Los Angeles, California*

The art of teaching is the art of assisting discovery.

MARK VAN DOREN, *American poet and editor*

Children are remarkable for their intelligence and ardor, for their curiosity, their intolerance of shams, the clarity and ruthlessness of their vision.

ALDOUS HUXLEY, *British writer*

For success in training children the first condition is to become as a child oneself, but this means no assumed childishness, no condescending baby-talk that the child immediately sees through and deeply abhors. What it does mean is to be as entirely and simply taken up with the child as the child himself is absorbed by his life.

ELLEN KEY, *Swedish writer and feminist*

The power to see the world in a strong, fresh and beautiful way is a possession of all children. And the desire to express that vision is a strong creative and educational force. If there is a barrier in its way . . . the teacher has to find a way to break that barrier down, or to circumvent it.

KENNETH KOCH, *American poet and teacher*

Men must be taught as if you taught them not;
And Things unknown propos'd as Things forgot.

ALEXANDER POPE, *British poet*

Always in our presentation we must give something which does not exceed the child's powers, and yet at the same time calls forth effort.

MARIA MONTESSORI, *Italian educator*

The greatest sign of success for a teacher . . . is to be able to say, "The children are now working as if I did not exist."

MARIA MONTESSORI, *Italian educator*

Children need models rather than critics.

JOSEPH JOUBERT, *French ethicist and essayist*

The influence of a genuine educator lies in what he is rather than in what he says.

OSWALD SPENGLER, *German philosopher*

He teaches not by speech
But by accomplishment.

LAO-TZU, *Chinese philosopher*

Choose as a guide one who you will admire more when you see him act than when you hear him speak.

SENECA, *Roman tutor of Nero*

A man who knows a subject thoroughly, a man so soaked in it that he eats it, sleeps it and dreams it—this man can always teach it with success, no matter how little he knows of technical pedagogy.

H. L. MENCKEN, *American journalist*

Example is the school of mankind, and they will learn at no other.

EDMUND BURKE, *Irish-born British politician and writer*

Teach by doing whenever you can, and only fall back upon words when doing it is out of the question.

JEAN-JACQUES ROUSSEAU, *French philosopher*

I hear and I forget.

I see and I remember.

I do and I understand.

Chinese proverb

Draw lines, young man, many lines, from memory or from nature; it is in this way that you will become a good artist.

JEAN-AUGUSTE-DOMINIQUE INGRES,

French painter, to his student, Edgar Degas, French painter and sculptor

Mistakes are, after all, the foundations of truth, and if a man does not know what a thing *is*, it is at least an increase in knowledge if he knows what it is *not*.

CARL JUNG, *Swiss psychiatrist*

All human errors are impatience, a premature breaking off of methodical procedure, an apparent fencing-in of what is apparently at issue.

FRANZ KAFKA, *German novelist*

Genius is only a greater aptitude for patience.

GEORGES-LOUIS LECLERC,
Comte de Buffon, French naturalist

The educator must above all understand how to wait; to reckon all effects in the light of the future, not of the present.

ELLEN KEY, *Swedish writer and feminist*

Education—whether its object be children or adults, individuals or an entire people—consists in creating motives.

SIMONE WEIL, *French mystic philosopher*

A student is not a professional athlete. . . . He is not a little politician or junior senator looking for angles . . . an amateur promoter, a glad-hander, embryo Rotarian, café-society leader, quiz kid or man about town. A student is a person who is learning to fulfill his powers and to find ways of using them in the service of mankind.

HAROLD TAYLOR, *American educator*

Mankind have been created for the sake of one another. Either instruct them, therefore, or endure them.

MARCUS AURELIUS, *Roman emperor and philosopher*

The teacher's art consists in this: To turn the child's attention from trivial details and to guide his thoughts continually towards relations of importance which he will one day need to know, that he may judge rightly of good and evil in society.

JEAN-JACQUES ROUSSEAU, *French philosopher*

I'll always remember my fifth-grade teacher, Marion McCarroll. He emphasized the need to be a good citizen—to read, think, and participate in one's world.

IRENE JACKSON, *Irving, Texas*

There is nothing which spreads more contagiously from teacher to pupil than elevation of sentiment: Often and often have students caught from the living influence of a professor a contempt for mean and selfish objects, and a noble ambition to leave the world better than they found it; which they have carried with them throughout life.

JOHN STUART MILL, *British economist and philosopher*

The true division of humanity is between those who live in light and those who live in darkness. Our aim must be to diminish the number of the latter and increase the number of the former. That is why we demand education and knowledge.

VICTOR HUGO, *French poet and novelist*

Education is the movement from darkness to light.

ALLAN BLOOM, *American educator and writer*

To live is to think.

CICERO, *Roman orator and philosopher*

When he enters our classroom there is an expectant hush, like the moment just after an orchestra conductor has raised the baton. Following a few remarks about the book for this week, he acknowledges students who will make brief presentations. He guides a discussion, sometimes speaking more himself, sometimes less. Stories, tears, quiet laughter, dignity, and respect lead us to a deeper sense of all that it means to be truly human. Author, teacher, and witness, Elie Wiesel is teaching us to remember, to bear witness, and to be better friends to one another.

PATRICIA HENKING, *Merrimack, New Hampshire*

To me the sole hope of human salvation lies in teaching.

GEORGE BERNARD SHAW, *Irish-born British dramatist*

The real community of man . . . is the community of those who seek the truth, of the potential knowers.

ALLAN BLOOM, *American educator and writer*

If you would be a real seeker after truth, it is necessary that at least once in your life you doubt, as far as possible, all things.

RENÉ DESCARTES, *French mathematician and philosopher*

If a man will begin with certainties, he shall end in doubts; but if he will be content to begin with doubts, he shall end in certainties.

FRANCIS BACON, *British philosopher and statesman*

The first key to wisdom is assiduous and frequent questioning.

PETER ABELARD, *French philosopher and theologian*

It is better to ask some of the questions than to know all of the answers.

JAMES THURBER, *American writer and cartoonist*

What is the most humorous answer you've ever gotten from a student?

I suggested to a class that they ought to concentrate so that they could do something meaningful with their lives and not end up working at McDonald's. "But that's what I want to do," a student replied.

Nora Gaffin Shore, Los Angeles, California

That the largest land mammal was a whale.

Esther Caldwell, Corpus Christi, Texas

When asked what major literary work is attributed to Don Miguel de Cervantes of Spain, the answer came back exactly as the student had heard it . . . Donkey Hoho.

Susan Soares, Bristol, Rhode Island

"Answers will vary." A student of mine heisted my teacher's manual and had copied down the answers. When it came time to go over them he raised his hand and gave me that answer in all seriousness.

Kristen Sturtevant, Rochester, New Hampshire

The questions which one asks oneself begin, at last, to illuminate the world, and become one's key to the experience of others.

JAMES BALDWIN, *American writer*

Some questions don't have answers, which is a terribly difficult lesson to learn.

KATHARINE GRAHAM, *American newspaper publisher*

If you feel that you have both feet planted on level ground, then the university has failed you.

ROBERT F. GOHEEN, *American educator*

There is no teaching until the pupil is brought into the same state or principle in which you are; a transfusion takes place; he is you, and you are he.

RALPH WALDO EMERSON, *American poet and philosopher*

I bid you lose me and find yourselves.

FRIEDRICH WILHELM NIETZSCHE,

German philosopher and poet

Every real teacher is myself in disguise.

RICHARD BACH, *American writer*

We think we learn from teachers, and we sometimes do. But the teachers are not always to be found in school or in great laboratories. Sometimes what we learn depends upon our own powers of insight.

LOREN EISELEY, *American anthropologist*

[The best that the] great teachers can do for us is to help us to discover what is already present in ourselves.

IRVING BABBITT, *American humanist and scholar*

All men who have turned out worth anything have had the chief hand in their own education.

SIR WALTER SCOTT, *Scottish poet and novelist*

The cardinal virtue of a teacher [is] to protect the pupil from his own influence.

RALPH WALDO EMERSON, *American poet and philosopher*

The true teacher defends his pupils against his own personal influence. He inspires self-distrust. He guides their eyes from himself to the spirit that quickens him. He will have no disciple.

AMOS BRONSON ALCOTT, *American educator and philosopher*

An educator never says what he himself thinks, but only that which he thinks it is good for those whom he is educating to hear.

FRIEDRICH WILHELM NIETZSCHE,
German philosopher and poet

When I transfer my knowledge, I teach. When I transfer my beliefs, I indoctrinate.

ARTHUR DANTO, *American essayist and educator*

Education is a kind of continuing dialogue, and a dialogue assumes . . . different points of view.

ROBERT M. HUTCHINS, *American educator*

The authority of those who teach is often an obstacle to those who want to learn.

CICERO, *Roman orator and philosopher*

To observe people in conflict is a necessary part of a child's education. It helps him to understand and accept his own occasional hostilities, and to realize that differing opinions need not imply an absence of love.

MILTON R. SAPIRSTEIN,
American clinical professor of psychiatry

Of course you will insist on modesty in the children, and respect to their teachers, but if the boy stops you in your speech, cries out that you are wrong and sets you right, hug him!

RALPH WALDO EMERSON, *American poet and philosopher*

Teachers, what has teaching taught you?

My students have taught me that we must never give up; we must struggle if necessary to accomplish our goals, even when they seem impossible. I witness the efforts of my students each day and I am in awe of them.
Lisa Hoganson, Delmont, New Jersey

Always have a great sense of humor and never take yourself too seriously.
Tina Moulton, Libertyville, Illinois

Sometimes it seems my most difficult students teach me the most—about patience, listening, compassion, trying harder, and tolerance.
Dawna Buchanan, Warrensburg, Missouri

I don't try to just push the curriculum. I let the students be my guide. Sometimes it's more important to be off-task for a few minutes—it's where the real lessons are frequently found.
Lynne Gibson, Elkins Park, Pennsylvania

I never reprimand a boy in the evening—darkness and a troubled mind are a poor combination.
Frank L. Boyden, American headmaster

When a student is worried about what is going on at home it's hard to get his or her mind totally on what you want them to learn. Some days it's more important to just be there and make their lives at school a pleasant experience.
Ann Marie Barket, Frackville, Pennsylvania

I student taught in an inner-city school. Those sixth and eighth graders taught me that even though they may act tough, they still want and need caring, warmth, and love.
Amy Giuffrida, Fogelsville, Pennsylvania

I am learning more and more that it is not as important to focus on the subject matter as it is to try and treat every student with respect, an open mind, and ultimately, an open heart. Let them know that you genuinely care about their success not only in your class, but in life.
Michele Hewson, Westfield, New Jersey

The teacher is no longer merely the one who teaches, but one who is himself taught in dialogue with the students, who in turn while being taught also teach.

PAULO FREIRE, *Brazilian educator*

Wherever there are beginners and experts, old and young, there is some kind of learning going on, and some sort of teaching. We are all pupils and we are all teachers.

GILBERT HIGHET, *Scottish-born American classicist*

I am a writer of books in retrospect. I talk in order to understand; I teach in order to learn.

ROBERT FROST, *American poet and teacher*

My joy in learning is partly that it enables me to teach.

SENECA, *Roman tutor of Nero*

To teach is to learn twice over.

JOSEPH JOUBERT, *French ethicist and essayist*

They know enough who know how to learn.

HENRY BROOKS ADAMS, *American historian*

Who dares to teach must never cease to learn.

JOHN COLTON DANA, *American librarian*

Anyone who stops learning is old, whether at twenty or eighty. Anyone who keeps learning stays young. The greatest thing in life is to keep your mind young.

HENRY FORD, *American automaker*

Leisure without study is death.

SENECA, *Roman tutor of Nero*

Whoso neglects learning in his youth, loses the past and is dead for the future.

EURIPIDES, *Greek dramatist*

Say not, When I have leisure I will study; perchance thou wilt never have leisure.

HILLEL THE ELDER, *Babylonian-born rabbi*

Learning is ever in the freshness of its youth, even for the old.

AESCHYLUS, *Greek tragic dramatist*

We have to abandon the idea that schooling is something restricted to youth. How can it be, in a world where half the things a man knows at 20 are no longer true at 40—and half the things he knows at 40 hadn't been discovered when he was 20?

ARTHUR C. CLARKE, *British writer*

We live in a time of such rapid change and growth of knowledge that only he who is in a fundamental sense a scholar—that is, a person who continues to learn and inquire—can hope to keep pace, let alone play the role of guide.

NATHAN M. PUSEY, *American educator*

A man who reviews the old so as to find out the new is qualified to teach others.

CONFUCIUS, *Chinese philosopher*

One looks back with appreciation to the brilliant teachers, but with gratitude to those who touched our human feelings. The curriculum is so much necessary raw material, but warmth is the vital element for the growing plant and for the soul of the child.

CARL JUNG, *Swiss psychiatrist*

If I could contact Mrs. Jacobsen today, I'd tell her that her care was the bright spot in my year.

MARTHA BROTHERS, *Fort Worth, Texas*

My favorite teacher was my fifth-grade teacher, Mrs. Locker. I was the silent, shy student at the back of the room. She believed I had something to say and would accept no less than my best.

AMY BONILLA, *Glendale, Arizona*

The best teacher I ever had was my sixth-grade teacher, Mrs. Kohut. Having moved to the U.S. from Trinidad, I'd been uprooted from all that I knew. It seemed to me she understood what I was going through. She took the time and made the effort to give me special attention and praise me as often as she could. Her attention helped me to overcome my shyness and insecurities.

AKLIMA BAKSH, *Plainfield, New Jersey*

In teaching you cannot see the fruit of a day's work. It is invisible and remains so, maybe for twenty years.

JACQUES BARZUN,
French-born American educator and historian

I'll always remember Miss Ancettia, she talked softly, and everyone loved her. We really listened when she spoke. She reinforced what my parents had told me. No need to raise your voice, only your consciousness.

STEPHENIE M. HOPE, *Los Angeles, California*

A teacher's major contribution may pop out anonymously in the life of some ex-student's grandchild.

WENDELL BERRY, *American poet and teacher*

Mrs. Irene Hettick, my biology teacher, always treated me with respect—even when I was fifteen years old and deciding to quit school. She just listened and told me if I ever changed my mind she would be there to help. I did quit school. When I finally decided to get my GED, I won a Teacher's Scholarship and wrote to her. She sent me money for my first quarter's textbooks.

SHARI MARSHALL, *Barry, Illinois*

Mrs. Kean taught us that if you succeeded in your academic studies and truly applied yourself, those "habits" would follow you later into life helping you achieve personal as well as professional success. It is a trait I have applied to my own life and have instilled in my children.

MERCEDES MALDONADO, *Jersey City, New Jersey*

I was still learning when I taught my last class.

CLAUDE M. FUESS, *American educator*

The teacher's task is not to implant facts but to place the
subject to be learned in front of the learner and, through
sympathy, emotion, imagination and patience, to awaken in
the learner the restless drive for answers and insights which
enlarge the personal life and give it meaning.

NATHAN M. PUSEY, *American educator*

We teachers can only help the work going on, as servants wait
upon a master.

MARIA MONTESSORI, *Italian educator*

The ability to think straight, some knowledge of the past,
some vision of the future, some urge to fit that service into the
well-being of the community—these are the most vital things
education must try to produce.

VIRGINIA GILDERSLEEVE, *American educator*

A teacher affects eternity; he can never tell where his influence stops.

HENRY BROOKS ADAMS, *American historian*